The Fable of Joseph and Aséneth

The Fable of Joseph and Aséneth

A Mystical Parable of the Soul Seeking God

BY

Moses of Aghel

FREELY ADAPTED
INTO ENGLISH VERSE BY

Robert Nixon

RESOURCE *Publications* · Eugene, Oregon

THE FABLE OF JOSEPH AND ASÉNETH
A Mystical Parable of the Soul Seeking God

Resource Publications
An Imprint of Wipf and Stock Publishers
199 W. 8th Ave., Suite 3
Eugene, OR 97401

www.wipfandstock.com

PAPERBACK ISBN: 978-1-6667-0844-8
HARDCOVER ISBN: 978-1-6667-0845-5
EBOOK ISBN: 978-1-6667-0846-2

06/15/21

My Beloved spoke, and said unto me,
"Rise up, my love! My fair one, come!
For, lo, the winter is over and the rains are passed.
New flowers now bloom on the earth,
the time of the singing of birds has come,
and the voice of the turtledove is heard in our lands."

—Song of Solomon, 2:10–12

Contents

Introduction

Comme deux anges que torture
Une implacable calenture,
Dans le bleu cristal du matin
Suivons le mirage lointain!

—Charles Baudelaire

The story of Joseph, which appears in the final portion of the book of Genesis, is one of the most beautiful and best-loved passages of all the Scriptures. It is not surprising, therefore, that various legends and embellished versions of the original narrative, or elements thereof, have emerged over the course of the centuries, in the Jewish, Christian and Islamic traditions. One such embellished version—which is of particular interest, significance and beauty—is presented in this volume in an English verse adaptation, together with prose translations of two other related texts.

Infused with all the tender sensitivity and lyricism of the *Song of Solomon*, it relates the meeting and relationship of Joseph, the son of the patriarch Jacob, with Aséneth, the daughter of Putiphar, a priest of the Egyptian city of Heliopolis (also known as On or Annu). The nucleus of the narrative is a single biblical verse, namely Genesis 41:45, which reads thus:

> *And Pharaoh gave to Joseph as his wife Aséneth, the daughter of Putiphar, a priest of Heliopolis. Then Joseph went out to the land of Egypt.*

While the work may be read simply as a piece of imaginative fiction, Aséneth—who soon becomes the story's central and most sympathetic character—may also readily be taken as an allegorical figure of the human soul, as it moves through different stages in its relationship to God. It begins with an innocent and complacent satisfaction with its own goodness and the enjoyment of joys and beauties of a merely earthly character. It is then awakened to a sense of higher realities and vaster and more noble possibilities. This awakening is symbolized in the narrative by Aséneth's initial encounter and infatuation with Joseph. This Joseph, however, soon abandons her, offering only a somewhat vague and not entirely satisfactory explanation. Indeed, a subtle hint of this dynamic may be readily perceived in the verse from Genesis quoted above.

Following this abrupt abandonment by her beloved, and after a period of desolation or a 'dark night of the soul', Aséneth (the figure of the soul) enters into an apophatic and even nihilistic stage, a *via negativa*. In this stage, she destroys her formerly cherished idols and renounces all earthly pleasures and joys. Perceptible and comprehensible things seem to be stripped of their meaning and savor, in the face of a God who seems remote, abstract and entirely inaccessible.

Finally, a subtly different Joseph, a transfigured or divinized "heavenly Joseph", appears to Aséneth, with whom she then rejoices for all eternity. It is pertinent to note that, in the Septuagint and the Vulgate versions of Genesis, Joseph is at one point assigned an Egyptian name meaning "Savior of the world," suggesting that he is an archetype or figure of a future Messiah:

> And Pharaoh changed his name, and gave to him a name
> in the Egyptian language, meaning Savior of the world.[1]

The final and consummate state of joy resulting from her mystical union with the "Savior of the world" is a type of synthesis, purification and apotheosis of all Aséneth's former spiritual experiences and desires, an encounter with the Divinity which is simultaneously both completely incarnational and wholly transcendent. They enjoy together a never-ending, celestial banquet, the description of which is replete with symbolic and hierophantic suggestions of the Christian Eucharist.

---

1. Gen 41:45 (translated from the Vulgate).

The principal source of the text of the fable is two ancient Syriac codices now held in the British Museum: the sixth or seventh century Codex Londinensis Add. 7190, fol. 319, and the twelfth century Codex Londinensis Add. 17202, fol. 10. The Syriac text, which is attributed to Moses of Aghel, describes itself as a translation from a Greek source. Indeed, a somewhat shorter Greek version is published in the 1723 *Codex Pseudepigraphus Veteris Testamenti, Tomus II* of Johannes Albert Fabricius. The manuscript source of this is identified as the Codex Barrocianus Graecus 148. The Greek version differs in several noteworthy particulars—most conspicuously, perhaps, in its lack of a happy ending.

The distinguished orientalist and scholar Gustav Oppenheim published a Latin translation of the Syriac text(s) in 1886, bearing the title *Fabula Josephi et Asenethae apocrypha e libro syriaco latine versa*. This very fine edition is furnished with a detailed critical apparatus, identifying and commenting on the numerous textual variants and ambiguities which are to be found, and supplying suggested readings for the several *lacunae* in the manuscripts. It is the translated text of the edition of Oppenheim which forms the basis of the present poetic adaptation.

The author (or translator) responsible for the Syriac version, Moses of Aghel (variously given as Aggel or Inghilene), lived during the sixth century. Aghel, where he was born, was a town nestled in the verdant and picturesque mountainous vistas to the north of the city of Diyarbakir, in the Kurdistan region of modern-day Turkey. He translated several works from Greek into Syriac, including significant writings of St. Cyril of Alexandria. Some sources recount that he served as an abbot for a monastery within the non-Chalcedonian or monophysite orthodox church, although this remains uncertain.

It is to be noted that the present rendition of the work into English verse is a very free adaptation rather than a strictly literal translation. Indeed, it aims more at fidelity to the overall structure, style and spirit of the narrative, and at the reproduction of the totality of mood and color, rather than at punctilious precision in particulars. The discipline of rhyme and meter, constitutive of and essential to the traditional English poetic forms cultivated here, invariably demands a certain wandering from the strait and narrow path of semantic exactitude into the less fettered but more fanciful realms of paraphrase and descriptive amplification, auxesis and ornamentation. Hopefully, such an approach serves not to obscure or obfuscate, but rather more effectively and more vividly to communicate the vision and intentions of the original author.

In addition to the verse adaptation of the principal Syriac version, a prose translation of the shorter and simpler but deeply poignant Greek version is included in the present volume; as well as a prose translation of another Syriac fragment, relating a very different, but no less wondrous and oneiric, version of the fair Aséneth's life story.

Each of these works has particular and profound beauties to offer to the contemporary reader. It is hoped that the adaptations and translations humbly presented herein may be found to be of interest and utility to the scholar, and of pleasant diversion to the intrepid explorer of literary curiosities. But it is hoped also, and more importantly perhaps, that it may furnish something (albeit merely an inaureoled bagatelle) of inspiration and insight for all those who seek glimpses of that ineffable spiritual and mystical truth—which is found only in the sacrament of redemptive, divine and deifying Love—that shines forth as an immortal and holy fire, not only in the holy pages of canonical Scripture, but in each and every genuinely inspired work of fiction and literary art.

Robert Nixon, osb
Abbey of the Most Holy Trinity,
New Norcia, Western Australia

I. A Verse Adaptation of the Syriac *Fable of Joseph and Aséneth,* by Moses of Aghel

Translator's Proem

The tale which in these pages
In verse shall now be told
Derives from ancient sources—
Yea, writings rare and old.

It takes the hero, Joseph,
Old Jacob's favorite son;
And then, by wit and whimsy,
Its story's web is spun.

Though it remains uncertain,
It was, it seems, composed
About the year five hundred—
As far as scholars know.

In Syriac 'twas written,
But firstly penned in Greek,
Then later turned to Latin;
And now this monk does seek

To offer it in English,
To render it in rhyme,
That thus this gentle fable
May help to pass thy time,

May serve as mild diversion;
And maybe something more—
For hidden in its shadows
Glints gold from wisdom's store . . .

1.

In ancient times in Egypt,
That land of sun-kissed sand,
When ruled the lordly Pharaoh,
With strong, imperious hand,

Arose rich years of plenty,
When harvests did abound,
When fruit from gracious orchards
Did flourish all around;

When Ceres, kindly mother,
The suckling earth did sate,
As, breeze-caressed, the wheatfields—
Gold oceans—undulate;

When played aeolian zephyrs
Upon the flaxen fields
And glebes, whose gleaming greenness
A countless harvest yields.

Such was the plan of Heaven;
That seven seasons should
Bestow in generous kindness
Abundant stores of good,

When date and pomegranate
And barley, corn and vine
Should grant with hand unstinting
Their bounty, full and fine,

And then, another seven
Long years of driest drought
Would follow in their footsteps—
Mean years, to pass without

The boon of fruitful foison
Or harvests fit and due,
As clouds held back their blessings
Of rains and cooling dew.

So would earth's fecund verdure
First wax, then come to wane;
The meads' smaragdine glory
Left parched for want of rain.

Thus in his hidden wisdom
Had Heaven's Lord decreed
Full seven years of plenty,
Then seven years of need.

Now, at this time in Egypt,
Where mighty Nile's floods run,
Where pyramids reach skyward
Towards a fiery sun,

There dwelt a man called Joseph,
Old Jacob's progeny,
Whose tale of woe and wonder
In Scripture's books you'll see.

From bonds of wretched thralldom,
By wisdom and by skill
Acquired he his freedom
And rose, at last, to fill

A place of noble status
In peerless Pharaoh's court;
His prudence and wise labor
High rank to him had brought.

And Pharaoh made him satrap
And shrieve of all his laws,
And gave to him the charge of
His treasuries and stores.

Then Joseph, through the Spirit,
Pursuant to God's will,
Resolved with ample rations
The granaries to fill,

To serve as wise provision
When famine's grasp drew near,
Which he foresaw in vision
As Truth-instructed seer.

It was thus that he ventured,
Led forth by prescient mind,
Through farms and fields and fiefdoms,
Intent to seek and find

The richest of the harvests
And choicest of the grain
Wherewith throughout the famine
All Egypt to sustain.

2.

So Joseph, ever thorough,
In plenty's first kind year,
Traversed the span of Egypt,
To places far and near.

Eventually he came to
A township broad and fair,
The city known as Ánnu,[1]
Of clear and clement air.

There dwelt within this city
A man called Pútiphar,
Whose noble reputation
Reached unto ears afar.

A priest he was, and learnéd
In Egypt's arcane lore;
Of wisdom and of riches
He had a princely store.

But dearer than his silver,
More precious than his gold,
He cherished but one daughter,
Two years and twenty old.

1. i.e. Heliopolis.

A lovely, gracious maiden,
Aséneth was her name,
The tidings of whose beauty
Spread far on wings of fame.

More splendid than the peacock,
More gentle than the dove,
Her eyes of violet splendor
Surpassed the stars above.

With luminance celestial,
Effulgence all divine,
Her face the sun transcended,
And did the moon outshine.

Her hair was black as midnight
Yet glowed like lustrous silk,
Her limbs like graceful columns,
Her throat as white as milk.

Her lips were red as ruby
Of deepest passion's fire,
Whose kiss the very Heavens
With ardor did desire.

Yet hoped such Heavens vainly,
Their wooings rendered naught;
For spurned she all the lovers
Who for her favors sought.

And proud of heart and haughty,
Rejoicing in her grace,

She kissed her mirror only,
Kept veiled her gorgeous face.

Yet men of every nation,
From highest prince to thrall,
Paid court to sweet Aséneth,
But she rejected all.

And even did the noble
Great heir to Egypt's crown,
The son of mighty Pharaoh,
Succumb to her renown.

He begged his royal father,
"O, grant to me this maid,
That thus her peerless beauty
Shall be to all displayed!

"For apt it is and fitting
That she should be my mate.
Superb is she, and perfect
To share my regal state."

Yet Pharaoh did refuse him,
"My son, I hear thy plea.
But love is never happy
Unless bestowed for free.

"And were I to compel her
To serve thee as thy wife,
Her heart would be resentful,
And robbed of joy, thy life!"

3.

Now, Pútiphar resided
Within a palace fine,
Whose walls with spangled marble
And cinnabar did shine.

And by his wondrous castle
There stood a tower high,
An edifice resplendent
Ascending to the sky.

Atop its lofty vertex,
Aséneth there did dwell,
Just as a star in Heaven
Or pearl within its shell.

Her dwelling had ten chambers;
The first, with walls of gold,
Adorned with many alcoves
Her cherished gods to hold,

The gods of the Egyptians,
Each carved from rarest stone—
Of topaz, diamond, opal,
And gems of names unknown.

Aséneth made devotions
With piety each day

And to her cherished idols
Neglected not to pray.

For though but gloaming shadows
Of true Divinity,
A glimpse her heart was granted
Of higher Light to see.

The second of her chambers
Bright candles did illume,
And all her radiant garments
Were held within this room.

There moon-like pearls abounded
With precious silver's sheen,
And robes of seric samite
In fine array were seen,

And diadems refulgent
With brass and bronze and blue,
And rings of glyptic metals
Of amethystine hue,

And aigrettes carved from turquoise
With hieroglyphs bedight,
Strange veils bespun by mages
From thaumaturgic light.

Such wonders served but slightly
Her beauty to enhance,
For truly none could add to
The charm of her mere glance.

Now, to the next room moving:
Lo, in this chamber third
Were kept a hoard of victuals
Of rarity unheard,

Yes, fruits and priceless spices
Of rare, ambrosial taste
In plenitude were gathered,
In lush array were placed;

There mangos beamed like beryl,
And guavas glowed with red
Wherewith Aséneth's beauty
By beauty might be fed.

And wines were there and nectars,
A dew-besprinkled crop,
Whose savors and whose flavors,
Indeed, whose merest drop

Enchants as balm most potent,
Nepenthe for all ills,
When, poured forth in libation,
Their vermeil liquid fills

Fine vessels wrought from jacinth
Or goblets made from glass,
To quell the flames of sorrow,
Make worries all to pass;

And vats replete with honey
Pressed forth by saffron bees,
Of sapors rich and dulcet,
And calm as amber seas.

4.

Remain still seven chambers,
Beneath that turret's roof,
Exempt from all pollution
And from the earth aloof.

These chambers were the dwellings
Of seven damsels fair,
Who served the svelte Aséneth
With love and tender care.

And all these maids were born on
That very year and day
On which was born Aséneth,
Companion to their play.

And each was truly lovely,
Of faultless form and face,
True odalisques of beauty,
True paragons of grace.

Yet none could ever rival
Their mistress's supreme
And nonpareil splendor,
Which equaled any dream

Yet dreamt by sprite or mortal,
By ifrit, fey or djinn,
And whether pure with virtue
Or dark with lust and sin!

As stars of azure Heaven
Which sable night unfurls,
So glowed with light exquisite
Aséneth's servant girls.

And, like her, all were virgins
And vowed to chastity;
Disdaining wedlock's fetters,
They chose the liberty

Of maidenly existence—
Like blossoms of the field,
Which flourish freely, never
To plough nor scythe to yield—

Just so, with neither children
Nor spouse as gyves to bind,
In pleasure and in leisure
Their joy supreme to find.

5.

Aséneth's maids,
A blithe brigade
With smiles arrayed,
Rare joys displayed!
Their spirits bade
That song be made—
That song be made,
Whilst flutes of jade,
With gems inlaid,
Be deftly played.

How graceful was
That song they made!
And these the thoughts
Its words conveyed:

Of none the wife,
We choose the life
Most free from strife,
With laughter rife!

With merry glee,
Supremely free,
Through purity
And chastity,

We shall disdain
Hard wedlock's chain,
All passion's pain,
All heartbreak's rain!

With souls kept light,
We'll take our flight
From sorrow's plight
And care's dark night,

Unburdened by
The ills that try,
Make hearts to sigh
And eyes to cry.

Like mirrored gleams
From crystal streams,
Our souls are clean:
Our lives, sweet dreams!

6.

Within Aséneth's dwelling,
Of windows there were three,
Through which could sunlight enter,
Through which her eyes could see

The scenic charms surrounding
Her dome's exalted heights,
Perceiving there in wonder
Bright day's pellucid sights.

One window opened northwards;
One, south; and one, due east,
And through this last, the largest,
Aurora's light, released

From tenebrous horizons,
Rose rutilant each morn,
Enrobed in gleaming glory,
Of hyalescent dawn.

The northward facing window
Diversion's use did serve,
For through its vitreous surface
Aséneth could observe

The varied streams of people
Who passed the palace by,

With nonchalant and placid
Insouciance of eye.

She saw, too, looking downwards
The lush and luscious grounds,
The gardens rich and fragrant,
And spreading all around

The palace's gilt tourelles
And white, marmoreal sides,
With ever-changing colors
As ran the times and tides.

Now showed rich reds and purples,
Then flourished blues and greens,
In verdant, vernal glory,
And opalescent sheens.

And fragrances abounded
In mists of blended scent,
As to the lyric breezes
Perfumes sublime were lent.

And attars strange and mystic
Enthralled the spell-bound nose,
Where climbed Dream's gracile ilex
And bloomed Love's sacral rose;

Where bright macaws and toucans
And pheasants, grave and proud,
In rainbow-tinct fluorescence,
Resounded fanfares loud,

Whilst blithely sang the skylark,
Soft cooed the pensive dove
Its odes of contemplation,
Its rhapsodies of love.

And rippling fountains poured forth
Their waters pure and blue,
Of lazulite liquescence,
Like nascent morning's dew.

And round this magic garden
Stood walls of quartz and sard,
Resistant to invaders,
Sheer, steep and strong and hard.

There two and twenty soldiers
A constant guard did keep,
Whose glaives were ever whetted,
Whose eyes did never sleep.

7.

Now Joseph sent a message
Inscribed with his own hand
To Pútiphar in Ánnu,
Whose graven writ did stand:

"O, greetings noble vassal
Of Pharaoh's royal heart!
The blessings of our monarch
To thee do I impart.

"I come to gather harvests
To fill the public barns,
Extracting from the surplus
Of villages and farms.

"But fain I would thee visit
To share a meal with thee,
To drink with thee the chalice
Of hospitality."

With joyful expectation
Read Pútiphar these words,
For Joseph's lauds and praises
He oft, in sooth, had heard.

He made his chateau ready
To entertain as guest

The wise and handsome Joseph,
Of potentates the best.

He summoned then his daughter
And spoke in kindly tone,
"Aséneth, O my dearest,
To thee is surely known

"That man was made for woman
And husband made for wife,
That thus, through procreation,
May run the rill of life!

"We shall receive but shortly
A guest of status high.
I ask that thou should view him
With pleasant, gracious eye.

"For he would be a husband
Most fitting unto thee.
O daughter, heed my counsel,
Act thou upon my plea!"

Replied to him Aséneth,
"O father, faugh and fie!
I shall not *ever* marry;
Much rather would I die!"

Then fled she to her tower
Where, locking fast her door,
She vowed in heart to stay as
A virgin ever more.

8.

Soon Joseph did arrive at
The palace of the great
And noble Pútiphar, where
He knocked upon the gate.

He thence was led, as guest, through
Imposing, spacious halls,
Bedecked with lustrous moonstones
And agate-crusted walls.

And Pútiphar did greet him
With honor and with awe,
"All hail, O prudent Joseph,
Thou voice of Pharaoh's law!

"I pray thee to be seated,
To take thou here thine ease,
In hopes that our poor service
May thy discretion please!

"Do quaff with us a goblet
And taste with us a dish,
And know that we shall give thee
Whatever thou may wish!"

Now at this time Aséneth,
Whilst hidden in her tower,

Had let her heart grow curious,
Succumbing to this power,

As so she through her window
Did peer with eager eye,
In order that this Joseph
More clearly she might spy.

And, lo, he was resplendent
With every manly grace,
His form erect and slender,
Whilst god-like was his face.

He rode upon a chariot
Of platinum and gold;
Heroic was the courage
Upon his visage bold,

And in his hand a scepter
And on his head a crown,
And to his gaze imperious
His minions all bowed down.

Yea, like a son of Heaven
Did Joseph then appear,
His flesh of burnished copper,
His eyes, as crystal, clear.

Aséneth looked in longing
Upon this vision blest,
And keenest admiration
Reluctantly confessed.

For then within her heart's depths
Was struck love's sudden spark,
As scintillant as lightning
Which rends the leaden dark.

Discarding her commitment
To lonely chastity,
She burned instead for Joseph,
His tender spouse to be.

"A fool was I, and hasty,"
She to herself did say,
"To let my proud perverseness
To rule me with its sway.

"For now my heart does tell me
To serve as Joseph's wife,
Would grant me much more pleasure
Than unwed, single life!"

9.

Whilst sat Aséneth gazing,
Enrapt with Joseph's sight,
Lo, Joseph's eyes perceived her
Atop her turret's height.

His glance she wholly captured,
His heart she'd captured, too,
For such was her great beauty
That but its fleeting view

Sufficed to plant the seeds of
The deepest, truest love,
Just like a spell descending
As kestrel on a dove,

Or like an arrow launched from
Capricious Cupid's bow,
A dart celestial bearing
To mortal hearts below

A spark of Aphrodite's
Illuminating fire,
Perfusing human hearts with
Sweet love's divine desire.

So Joseph spoke up boldly;
To Pútiphar he said,

"Mine host, bestow this favor:
To me let now be led

"The maid in yonder window
Whom now my eye does see.
For fain am I to meet her.
Beseech I this of thee!"

And Pútiphar replied thus:
"The maid whom you behold
Is truly my own daughter,
Now twenty-two years old.

"I'll bring her to thy presence
That she thyself may greet,
And thus two hearts most noble
May fittingly here meet."

So summoned he his daughter,
Who quickly did appear
Before the mighty Joseph,
Aquiver, meek with fear;

With fear, indeed, but mixed with
The deepest of delight
To make the sweet acquaintance
Of Joseph, whose mere sight

Her heart and soul had captured
With love's soft, silken snare,
A man of gait majestic
And countenance most fair.

Once led before his presence,
She fell upon her knees
And homage duly paid him,
And quoth, "My Lord, O please,

"Accept me as thine handmaid;
Thy blessings to me give,
And joyfully hereafter
For love of thee, I'll live.

"And let thy God be *my* God,
For truly, it must be
That such a God as *thy* God
Claims true Divinity!"

This speech of adulation
Did Joseph's heart remind
Of God, and of his duties
To search out and to find

Rich grain for life's provisions,
Sound produce to collect.
His conscience then admonished
His stooping to neglect

High Heaven-given duties.
He mused and struck his chest,
"Too long here have I tarried,
Too freely taken rest!

"Forsooth, I must proceed now,
Continue with my work,

Lest tempted by mere beauty
God's calling I should shirk!"

To be of love disdainful
Had Joseph long been taught,
Within religion's strictest,
Unbending school of thought.

Thus he his heart mistrusted,
Lest it should lead astray
From holy laws unchanging,
From God's strait, narrow way.

So speaking words of blessing,
He gently bade adieu;
"Alas, I must depart now,
My duties to pursue.

"Aséneth, kindly sister,
My new but cherished friend,
I pray that Heaven's Caliph
To thee all blessings sends."

And softly did he kiss her
And chastely, on the hand.
He knelt in humble homage,
Then, once again, did stand.

With formal valedictions,
He promptly took his leave:
Left Pútiphar, bewildered;
Aséneth, left to grieve.

10.

Thence Joseph then proceeded,
Went forth upon his way,
To span the land of Egypt,
To search both night and day

For food and sound provender
With all care to be stored,
To save the folk from famine
And thus to serve his Lord.

But in her silent tower
Aséneth's heart sank low,
By melancholy taunted
And struck a bitter blow.

For though but once she saw him,
And though their parley brief,
Her Joseph's quick departure
Had fixed on her deep grief.

His coming seemed a vision,
A phantom of the night,
Which in the cold of morning
Must take its hasty flight.

The wise declare that beauty
Must ever fade away,

That mortal joy is passing,
Enduring but one day.

Yet to the maid Aséneth
Sore grievous did it seem
That her most comely Joseph
Should vanish as a dream.

So bode she in her chamber
And lay she on her bed,
With silent sighs and moaning,
Salt streams of tears she shed;

Oh, cried she then a river
Which seemed unchecked to flow,
And cried she then an ocean
Which seemed no shore to know.

And all her food refusing,
Her face was rendered pale,
And sleeping not nor resting,
Her strength began to fail.

Her servant girls entreated,
"O Mistress, what doth thee
Afflict in such a manner,
As visibly we see?

"Thy face, but late so radiant,
Thine hair, which did so shine,
Now fade like withered blossoms,
To sink and to repine;

"Or like the orb selenic,
Whose plenilunar light
Now wanes to almost nothing,
A slither in the night.

"Do tell us what afflicts thee
Or what torments thee so?
With kindness we'll assist thee,
Should we the cause but know."

Their mistress would not answer,
Nor furnish a reply,
Except to stare forth blankly
And silently to cry.

11.

Aséneth's heart
Felt pain's sharp smarts,
Which Love's cruel dart
So oft imparts.

A waning moon,
A darkened noon—
She happened soon
This dirge to croon
To sorrow's dull
And dreary tune,
To sorrow's dull
And restless tune:

O woe is me,
That I should see
Such quenchless seas
Of misery!

My eyes do cry,
My heart doth sigh,
My spirits die;
I wonder why

My Joseph fled?
By what force led,

He left me dead
On heartache's bed?

My quick is cut,
My soul is shut
Within this rut,
For I am but

An unstrung lute,
A broken flute,
A withered shoot,
A vain pursuit,

A blighted rose
Which no more shows
Love's blood-red glows
Or passion's mauves,
Nor to the nose
Sweet scent bestows;

And naught does know
But pain's black blow;
Yea, sinks now low
Beneath pain's blow,
Pain's cruel and black
And bitter blow.

12.

With passing time, Aséneth,
Submerged in gloomy dark,
Was struck as if by lightning's
Fierce, fulminating spark.

She called to mind her Joseph's
Great God of matchless might,
Who bears no name but I-AM
And hides in eldren height,

The God who needs no temple
Nor consecrated place,
Whose realm is light eternal
Beyond all time and space.

And for the sake of Joseph
She loved his Deity,
A God of void and silence,
Whom none could touch nor see.

So broke she all her idols;
She cast them to the floor,
The idols rich and splendid,
Which once she did adore.

She hurled them from her windows
In sacrilegious scorn,

The ancient cults denying
To which she had been born.

She crushed the gods of nature
The sprites of stars and moon;
She mocked the wraith of evening
And cursed the nymph of noon.

She trampled on the spirits
Of music, wine and love,
Renouncing earthly pleasures
For Him-who-dwells-above.

This unseen God enthralled her,
The Darkness with no name,
The all-embracing Nothing,
This anodyne for pain.

Yet, Pútiphar, all-patient,
When seeing her strange deeds,
Did weep like to a Father
Who bears a heart that bleeds,

That bleeds for its own daughter
Or Son, with pangs unknown,
Who feels the other's torments
As if they were his own,

As if they were his own, like
Sharp nails which pierce and tear,
With pain of crucifixion,
With Love's acerbic care . . .

13.

So, sunk in gloom's penumbra,
Aséneth did despair,
And lurked within her tower
As in a wild beast's lair;

Or oyster, eremitic
Within its petrous shell;
Or as a genie fettered
By warlock-uttered spell;

Or as a cold cadaver
In serpent-guarded tomb;
Or as a soul made heavy
By dread, despair and doom.

Her new-found faith in God seemed
Like darkness more than light,
Her piety like madness
Once reason's taken flight.

Yet then there came a vision—
And who can say if born
Of God or anxious sorrow,
Of midnight or of dawn?

Lo, through her orient window
She saw an aureate glow

Whose golden luminescence,
First faint, did wax and grow,

Until a sun had risen—
No earthly Phoebus this,
For all its light was happy
And all its rays were bliss,

With living warmth made vibrant,
Aflame did it resplend
With depths of animation
Which seemed to know no end.

And drew it ever nearer,
Approaching yet more nigh,
Until its fulgent presence
Engulfed both earth and sky.

Eventually before her
It stopped and took its place,
A human form assuming,
And bearing human face.

Yea, like unto a human,
A mortal man most fine,
But something more than human,
Somehow, indeed, divine.

This man resembled Joseph
In countenance and mien,
And yet displayed a difference
More subtly felt than seen.

His form was surely similar,
Symmetrical and brave,
Yet stronger, too, and kinder,
More gentle and more grave.

And spoke he to Aséneth,
"My child, forfend to fear,
For I am as thy brother
And thou to me art dear.

"My name I shall not utter,
For wonderful it be.[2]
I come, though, for one purpose,
To be but loved by thee;

"To be but loved sincerely,
As thee my heart does love,
Since first thy face I saw from
My Kingdom up above.

"Oh, from my realm sidereal
Descended I below,
Since, whilst I dwelt in Heaven,
My face I could not show.

"But I perceive thee hungry
And fain that thou be fed,
Though naught have I to offer
Except my wine and bread."

2. See Judg 13:8.

And then appeared a supper,
Gold bread and scarlet wine,
On which the fair Aséneth
With her new host did dine.

And, lo, the bread was wholesome
Yet seemed like unto flesh,
And blood-like was the wine which
Her soul, with grace, refreshed.

Their discourse was most holy
And chaste and pure and true,
Of limpid fascination,
With wonders always new.

This feast was long extended
And ever grew more fine,
The bread and wine more living,
Its bounty more divine.

This feast became a Heaven,
From every sorrow free,
Which, ending not, continues
For all eternity . . .

14.

In raptures best
These twain still rest,
Their love confessed
With ardent zest.
O, deeply blest
Their timeless rest!

And glow the fires
Of fierce desires,
Ascend their pyres
Yet ever higher,
Whilst ring the lyres
Of angel choirs,
In wondrous song
Which Love inspires:

Aséneth fair!
How dark thy hair,
How warm thy stare,
Aséneth fair!

How soft thy sighs,
How deep thy eyes
In which does rise
High glory's prize!

Thou lily white,
Thou radiant sight:
Thou comet bright
Whose lucent light
Doth conquer night;
Yea, conquers swart
And pard-hued night,
With glints of pearl
And chrysolite.

Thou mystic dream
Of joy supreme!
Thou golden gleam
Of beauty's beam!

Thy every glance
Makes stars to dance,
And God's own gaze,
Yea, does entrance.

Thine every kiss
Is perfect bliss!
Yes, Heaven's own
Most perfect bliss
Is surely this—
Thine every kiss!

15.

Then poured forth yet another
Delightful wave of singing,
To fair Aséneth bringing
New ecstasies of joy,

And Time and Space, both joining,
In harmony united,
By fire celestial lighted,
Did all their pow'rs employ:

Behold the moon, Aséneth!
From welkin zeniths glowing,
Its argent fulgors showing
Through far, purpureal skies.

Behold its distant shining,
Perceive its gentle glimmers,
Its undulating shimmers,
Reflected in thine eyes.

Aséneth, Queen thrice-holy!
Behold the planets gleaming,
In tranquil slumber dreaming,
As now they wander by;

As ever-yearning spirits,
Inflamed with ardor fervent,

All surge with longings urgent;
Each breathes its heart-felt sigh.

To thee they call, Aséneth!
They long for thee to hear them,
And hope thou'll linger near them,
In astral meads above.

A chorus of the angels
Now sings thy ceaseless praises,
As to the heights it raises
New dithyrambs of love,

In seas of purest aether—
A mirrored, nacreous ocean,
Which heaves in gyrant motion
To bathe yon moon-kissed shore.

To thee, a tender love-song
Is crooned in gentle nearness,
Its notes of chime-like clearness
To echo evermore.

The scions of the Heavens,
And high elysian powers,
Collect for thee rare flowers
From swards of starry space.

To thee, bow down, adoring,
These potentates supernal,
With words of love eternal,
Entranced by thy sweet face.

Divine now is thy Joseph,
To whom in love thou flyest:
He's crowned with glory highest,
As God's own truest Son!

To him thou art betrothed now,
In mystical communion,
In hypostatic union:
With God, forever one!

16.

But back in realms telluric,
In earthly time and space,
Not ought of this appeared, where
Such wonders held no place.

Instead, did sable torpor
And silence seem to keep
The wan Aséneth's soul in
A state akin to sleep.

So Pútiphar grew anxious,
As did each servant maid,
For locked within her chamber
Aséneth long had stayed.

For days and nights full seven
No sound had been perceived,
No visitant accepted,
No food nor drink received.

So forced they now to open
The room where she had been,
Yet empty was that parlor,
No Mistress to be seen.

Yes, of her lovely presence
Her chamber was bereft;
Of soul and mortal body
No trace nor shade was left.

There lingered, though, an odor,
A scent of sanctity,
The fragrant breath of Heaven,
Of pure serenity.

And lay a moon-white lotus
Upon Aséneth's bed,
And deeply did they ponder
To where she may have fled,
Or whither she'd been led,
If living or if dead . . .

17.

The mortal man named Joseph,
Who duty did pursue,
Rose steadily in honor;
But, in due course, he grew

Less youthful and less handsome,
More firm and stiff and strong,
More expert in his business,
More sure of right and wrong.

And Love he scarce remembered,
Aséneth's name forgot,
His wine he took in measure;
He laughed and jested not.

His coat of many colors
He cared no more to wear;
His dreams and mystic visions
He dared no more to share.

His hair turned silver; faded
The fire within his eye,
And, as all flesh is destined,
Grew old; at last, to die.

Thus ashes turn to ashes
And dust returns to dust

And light to brumal shadows,
As gold decays to rust.

Grow dull the coruscations
Of summer's fleeting day,
To shades of sallow winter,
To sullen, dreary gray;

Yea, fades and fades away,
And pales to ashen gray
The ever-dying day,
Life's chill and dreary day
Upon its weary way,
Enrobed in glaucous gray,
In cold, cinerious clay,
In dread and dark dismay—
Life's tired and futile day,
Which wends its weary way,
To fade, and fade away . . .

18.

But somewhere up in Heaven
Two souls rejoice in bliss,
Their union consecrated
By Love's ensorcelled kiss.

And one is called Aséneth,
The Other's name, unknown—
And both now dwell forever
Within their star-lit home,

In lambent waves of glory
In plains of sapphire light,
In which commingle sweetly
Rich pleasures of the night

With day's cerulean splendor;
And where, in joy, combine
The human heart's warm passions
With purest joys divine;

And crystal, Lethean rivers
Of Eden's waters flow,
And amaranthine arbors
With emerald verdure grow,
And flames of Love immortal
In deathless rapture glow.

My friends, let us remember
This legend old and true,
Of beautiful Aséneth
And righteous Joseph, too.

This story has no moral
Nor lesson to convey,
Except that Heaven loves those
Who Love's high Law obey.

To God be endless glory,
Who reigns enthroned above,
Who shines with light eternal,
And lives in holy Love;
Yea, lives not anywhere
Except in holy Love.

Amen.

II. A Prose Translation of the Greek
Life of Aséneth, the Wife of Joseph

Just as a thirsting deer panteth for the streams of flowing water,
Even so doth my soul long for thee . . .

—Psalm 42:1

1.

In the first year of the seven years of plenty which fell upon the land of Egypt in ancient times, Pharaoh sent forth his trusted minister, the Hebrew, Joseph, the favorite son of Jacob, to gather grain for storage as provision for the seven years of dire famine which were predicted to follow. And in the course of this mission, Joseph came into the great and stately city of Heliopolis. Now, the leader of this city was a most noble and illustrious man called Putiphar, who was a venerated priest and erudite mysteriarch of the sun-god, Amun, and head of the satraps and high counsellors of Pharaoh.

Putiphar had a daughter named Aséneth, whose wondrous beauty surpassed that of all the maidens on earth, of all the houris of Paradise, and even of the very angels in Heaven. In her golden complexion and symmetrical and well-curved features, she looked rather like one of the women of the Hebrews. But Aséneth, though lovely in appearance, was haughty and proud in character, and regarded all men with uniform and consummate disdain. And no person of the masculine gender, apart from her father and the members of her own household, had ever once set eyes upon the divinely beautiful and singularly enchanting aspect of this girl.

Beside the palace of Putiphar there was constructed a lofty and magnificent tower, at the top of which was a spacious apartment having ten chambers. The first of these chambers was lined with polished porphyry of purest purple, and its walls were decorated with sparkling, polychromatic gemstones of flawless clarity, and paneled with sheets of iridescent madreperl and beaten electrum and orichalch. Within this chamber were kept images of all the deities of the Egyptians, fashioned from glistening gold and refined silver. And each day, Aséneth would offer sacrifices of pious prayer and fragrant incense to this pantheon of idols, paying humble homage with all reverence and devotion, according to the ancient and time-honored traditions of the Egyptians.

2.

The second chamber in the tower served as the holding place for Aséneth's precious jewelry and garments, which were of a splendor and magnificence which exceeded all calculable price. The third chamber served to hold the victuals for Aséneth and her companions. These consisted of the rarest of fruits and most delectable of nectars; with berries of crimson and coquelicot, and melons of indigo and icterine, as well as wines of opalescent tints of shimmering amber and burning vermillion, amassed in boundless bounty, and profuse in perfect plenitude.

The remaining seven chambers each served as accommodation for seven especially chosen maidens. These youthful women were both servants and companions to Aséneth. Each of them was of such exquisite beauty that it may scarcely be described by any human words; and none had ever conversed with, or even been seen by, a man or a male youth.

In the bedroom of Aséneth herself, there were three fine and expansive windows, each of surpassing clarity. The first was very large. It faced the east, admitting daily the golden light of the rising sun. The second faced to the south, while the third faced to the north.

In this chamber was a luxurious bed covered in cloth of richest purple, lavishly flecked with spun gold. It was in this marvelous bed that the beauteous maiden Aséneth took her slumber. And truly, she slept there always alone and always untroubled. For, indeed, never once had any man at all dared to enter, or even to cast his eyes upon, the private dwelling place of this woman of celestial and awesome beauty.

Moreover, around Aséneth's tower, there was a vast courtyard, enclosed by bulwarks of immense height and adamantine hardness, constructed from impenetrable blocks of hewn basalt, as black and opaque as a moonless night. And within these protective walls were four gates of solid iron, diligently guarded by some eighteen brave warriors, each youthful and mighty, and armed with gleaming and keenly-sharpened scimitars. The courtyard contained a gorgeous fountain from which flowed continuously streams of sparkling, crystalline waters. And these waters irrigated the delightful gardens planted therein, which consisted of trees adorned with rainbow-colored and fragrant flowers of fresh and fertile fruitfulness, and vines and arbors of luminous and magical verdancy.

As for Aséneth herself, she was verily as magnificent as Sarah, the wife of Abraham; and truly as beautiful as Rebecca, the wife of Isaac; and as flawlessly and alluringly shapely as Rachel, the wife of Jacob and the mother of Joseph.

3.

Joseph, having arrived in the city of Heliopolis, sent a message to Putiphar, the high priest, that he would like very much to visit him. Putiphar was delighted to hear this message, and sent for his daughter Aséneth. He told her that Joseph was known to be a fine man and a pious votary of God, and that he dearly hoped that Joseph would be persuaded to accept Aséneth as his wife.

Upon hearing this, the proud Aséneth was filled with indignation. Defiantly she retorted that she would never consider such a man—whom she regarded as a mere foreign factotum, a servant or slave—as a potential husband, but would contemplate no one less than the first-born son of a sovereign king to be her future spouse.

While Putiphar and Aséneth were speaking thus, Joseph himself suddenly entered into the grounds of their palace, with great fanfare and awesome splendor. He was borne upon a golden chariot, drawn by four identical horses of whiteness resembling purest snow, each harnessed by reins fashioned from gleaming, precious metals. Joseph was clad in a radiant tunic of dazzling white, with a robe of imperial purple draped upon his broad shoulders. On his head was an imposing diadem, adorned with twelve magnificent gemstones and twelve stars fashioned from brightly polished gold. And in one hand he held a gilded scepter of royal power, and in the other hand a graceful olive branch, heavily laden with its sumptuous fruit.

4.

Putiphar, together with his wife, respectfully approached their guest, Joseph; whilst Aséneth, surprised and alarmed, fled to her tower. Kneeling and bowing low, Putiphar and his wife greeted Joseph with all homage and veneration. He then accompanied them into the hall of their wonderful dwelling, and the heavy outer gates of the palace were closed.

At this point, Aséneth beheld Joseph from the window of her tower, and her heart suddenly stirred uncontrollably within her, like a startled lark about to take its flight. She exclaimed, "Lo! The Sun himself has come down from Heaven in his golden chariot! Indeed, little did I realize that this Joseph was verily a son of God; for who amongst the offspring of mere mortals could possibly bear the superlative quintessence of beauty and magnificence which he so abundantly possesses? Who, out of all those born of women, could possibly display such incomparable radiance as shines forth boldly from his eyes, like the very fire of Heaven?"

And, as Aséneth gazed upon him from her window, Joseph entered the house of the high priest, Putiphar. And Putiphar humbly washed Joseph's feet, as a token of welcome and honor.

5.

As Joseph was graciously received into the house of Putiphar in this manner, he caught a glimpse of Aséneth, as she herself gazed upon him from the heights of her tower. And he enquired, "Pray tell me, who is that graceful damsel whom I can see through the window of the tower—appearing, indeed, as the silver moon of summer shining through the translucent grayness of the enveloping clouds?"

Now, despite her overwhelming admiration for Joseph, Aséneth did not come down to meet him at once. For she sensed that many beautiful and noble women must surely have eagerly and boldly solicited his attention already, and she had no wish to annoy him by becoming yet one more amongst this number.

Meanwhile, Putiphar answered Joseph's question, "My Lord, the maiden whom you see through the window is my own unmarried daughter, Aséneth. But I must tell you that she views all men with equal contempt and disdain. Indeed, no man has ever seen her face, except for myself—and now, from today, you also! But if you wish, I shall command her to come down from her tower and greet you."

Joseph thought to himself that if Aséneth regarded all men with disdain and contempt, she was not likely to vex him with any amorous intentions. And so he said to Putiphar, "If this girl is your daughter, then I shall regard her as a true sister to myself! So, please, bring her forth, that I may meet her."

And, upon hearing this, Aséneth's mother went to the tower, and promptly brought her beautiful daughter into the presence of Joseph.

6.

Once Aséneth stood before Joseph, her father addressed her, "My daughter, salute your new brother! For just as you are not interested in the attention of any man, so he likewise is not interested in the love of any woman."

And Aséneth greeted Joseph thus: "O Hail, thou who art blessed by the most high God of Heaven!" And Joseph replied, "May that same God, who is the one source of all life, bless you abundantly!"

And Putiphar then instructed his daughter to give to Joseph a sisterly kiss of respect and honor. Upon hearing this, Aséneth's heart burned within her, for she dearly longed to kiss Joseph. Yet he raised his powerful hand and gently but firmly stopped her, saying, "It is not fitting that I, a man who worship the true and living God, should be kissed by the unclean lips of a woman who worships vain idols of stone and wood! It is not fitting that I, a man who eat of the bread of eternal life and drink of the chalice of everlasting salvation, should be kissed by the polluted lips of a woman who eats of the foul and fetid bread of idolatry and drinks of the vile and venefic chalice of falsehood!"

7.

When Aséneth heard these words from Joseph, she was struck by a profound sadness and wept bitterly and profusely. But Joseph immediately felt pity for the maiden, and placed his hand upon her head and blessed her. At the touch of his hand and his blessings, Aséneth was filled with ineffable joy. And quite overcome with confused emotions, she rushed out immediately to the refuge of her tower. There she threw herself upon her bed, weak and pale with excitement.

And, as she looked around her chambers, she regretted that she had ever worshipped the deities of the Egyptians. Filled with love for Joseph and love for his unknown God, she renounced her idols of silver and gold as either false and fictitious deceptions, or impure and odious demons.

Meanwhile, Joseph ate, drank and conversed with Putiphar and his wife. Then, suddenly rising, he advised them that he was obliged to make his departure forthwith. Putiphar urged him to stay for another day, but he declined to do so, as his work required his immediate attention elsewhere. He undertook to return, however, once his current business in the region was completed; and promised to visit them again in eight days.

8.

Upon Joseph's departure, Aséneth's heart was filled with the blank darkness of oppressive grief. Now it had happened that her younger brother had died some time before the events related herein transpired. Aséneth took the black mourning garment which she had worn for her deceased brother, and garbed herself once more in the veils of its ebon melancholy.

She locked the door of her chambers firmly, then proceeded to hurl all her former idols from the window which opened to the north, with scorn and disdain. And she took all the luxurious viands with which she was provided, and cast these contemptuously through another window to be eaten by the hungry dogs who prowled the courtyard below. And she smeared her lovely face with ashes, and wept most bitterly—with neither respite nor intermission—for the space of seven long days and nights, awaiting the return of her beloved Joseph . . .

III. A Prose Translation of the Syriac Narration of *The Life of Aséneth*

Oft indeed has the question been posed to us: "What is the story of the lovely Aséneth—that maiden of legendary beauty!—who was the wife of the most handsome and noble patriarch Joseph?" Hearken now, O my friends, and lend to me your attentive ears! For we shall now narrate the venerable and ancient story of Aséneth, which we have learnt from the wisdom of the wise, and gleaned from the secret sayings of the sages.

* * *

In the times of the patriarch Jacob, a certain Hivite man called Sichem committed fornication with one of the daughters of Jacob, Dinah.[3] This Dinah was the sister of Jacob's many sons—the future patriarchs of the nation of Israel—who included Simeon and Levi.

Now it came to pass that Jacob suspected that his daughter Dinah was with child by Sichem, and he secretly apprised his sons Simeon and Levi of the situation. These two zealous young men, the sons of Jacob and the brothers of Dinah, were, naturally, infuriated. They determined to set out and destroy the city of which Sichem was a citizen, slaughtering all its inhabitants with the edge of the sword, from the greatest unto the very least. Moreover, suspecting their sister Dinah of being pregnant with Sichem's illegitimate child, they threatened her thus: "If it should happen that you give birth to a child—the bastard seed of your fornication with this accursed Hivite—we will surely not hesitate to kill both you and the infant!"

As the time for Dinah to give birth to her child drew nigh, she became terrified on account of her brothers' most cruel and violent threats. So, to escape from them, she fled into the desert and hid herself in the inhospitable wastes of its bleak and silent

---

3. See Gen 34.

solitude. And there she gave birth to her baby—a tiny girl-child. She tenderly wrapped the delicate child in swaddling clothes, and gently placed her beneath the shade of a thorn bush for protection against the scorching intensity of the desert heat. And there she stood by, mourning and weeping in the disconsolate anguish of hopeless and lonely despair.

But then—behold!—a great and majestic eagle of golden plumage suddenly appeared on the horizon, soaring in mighty flight in the empty and pallid azure of the limitless desert sky. Now, this magnificent eagle had its domicile in the land of Egypt, and was fed there by the daily sacrifices made to the sun-god, Amun. From the heights of the firmament where it hovered, the formidable bird perceived the tiny girl-child, the daughter of Dinah.

And swooping down, it seized the helpless infant in its powerful talons and carried it off. Swift indeed was its flight as it quickly traversed the vast expanses of space! And very soon did it arrive back in its homeland of Egypt. And once there, it gently placed the baby girl upon the altar of the god, Amun. The mother, Dinah, had seen her child being seized and carried away by the great gold-winged eagle. But as to where she had been taken, she had not the slightest inkling . . .

* * *

Now in Egypt at that time, there resided a most noble and learned priest of Amun in the city of Heliopolis, who was called Putiphar. And it happened that, just as the eagle had placed the daughter of Dinah upon the altar of Amun, Putiphar went to make his customary ritual offerings of incense to the god whom he served. He perceived upon the altar the baby, and was filled with astonishment; and, in alarm, rushed back to his house with flustered alacrity.

When Putiphar's wife saw him back from his sacerdotal duties so soon, she was surprised and asked him, "Pray tell, how is it that you have returned so early from the temple today?" He replied, "Forsooth, I have beheld this day an utterly new and unprecedented miracle from the gods! The Heavens have now given birth to a child. For when I entered the temple, the gates thereof were all firmly locked, according to custom. Yet there lay upon the altar of Amun a small infant, verily a miraculous child!"

Then the couple both arose and together went to the temple. And they saw there the infant upon the altar, and also the eagle with it. This great and majestic bird sat lovingly by the baby with its tremendous wings stretched over it, as if protecting it. Then both Putiphar and his wife understood that it was the eagle—the bird sacred to the solar deity—who had carried the girl-child and placed it upon the altar of Amun.

The wife of Putiphar at once took the child, and assigned it to a nurse to be cared for. Since the couple themselves had not been blessed by any offspring—having neither a son nor a daughter—they gladly welcomed this opportunity to adopt the unknown and miraculous child as their very own, giving her the name Aséneth.

Indeed, Putiphar and his wife dearly loved the girl and cherished her with the deepest affection. And she grew up into a young woman of truly astonishing beauty. Putiphar had constructed for her a magnificent dwelling place, in which she could live with a group of beautiful virgins, who served her as devout handmaids and companions. And many of the sons of kings and caliphs, of sultans and sovereigns, of princes and potentates, of earls and emirs, earnestly besought her flawless and shapely hand in sacred matrimony. For she indeed surpassed all other women in beauty and grace and splendor, and equally excelled in wisdom and gentleness. Fair indeed was she, beyond all the dreams and desires of the mortal heart! But Aséneth looked upon all her suitors with unvarying and uncompromising disdain. She displayed to none of them any sign of favor, preference, affection or approval.

* * *

In those days, Joseph, the son of Jacob, who had been sold by his brothers into slavery, had risen to great prominence and power in the Kingdom of Egypt, by virtue of his merit and industry. All the people spoke most favorably of his outstanding wisdom, strength and ability. Indeed, contrary to her usual custom of scorning all men, even the beauteous Aséneth came to regard this foreigner with profound and sincere admiration.

Now Pharaoh, the king, had grown weary with the exercise of royal power, and so resolved to appoint Joseph, in whom he had the utmost confidence and trust, as his chief minister and high vizier. He accordingly appointed him to this exalted rank, and command- ed that a seal of imperial power be given to the young Hebrew, and that a royal ring of purest gold be placed on his right hand. Fur- thermore, Pharaoh commanded that Aséneth, the daughter of the high priest Putiphar—who was reputed to be the most beautiful and gracious maiden in all of Egypt—should be given to Joseph as his wife. And both Joseph and Aséneth were delighted at Pharaoh's decision and decree regarding their union, and so became a very happy couple indeed—she, the loveliest of all women; and he, the strongest and most handsome of men.

* * *

In due course, the elderly patriarch Jacob, the father of Joseph, came to visit his favorite son in Egypt. And his daughter, Dinah—the same one whose child had been borne away by the eagle in the desert many years before—accompanied him. Both Jacob and Dinah went to the palace of Joseph and Aséneth and were brought into their presence, saluting them warmly and respectfully.

After Dinah had greeted her brother Joseph, she turned to his wife Aséneth. And as Dinah gazed upon Aséneth's face, her heart began to burn within her inexplicably. She asked her, "Pray tell me, most honored lady, of whom are you the daughter?" Asé- neth replied, "I am the adopted daughter of Putiphar, the chief of the priests of Amun, the god of the Sun." She then went on to narrate the wondrous story of how she had been placed upon the altar of the temple by the eagle, whilst still wrapped in swaddling clothes. Upon hearing this story, Dinah enquired if Aséneth still, perchance, had these swaddling clothes in her possession. She replied in the affirmative, and at once had them brought in to their presence.

Dinah inspected them closely and intently, and immediately recognized them as the very same ones in which she had wrapped her own infant. She then understood that Aséneth, the wife of her beloved brother Joseph, was, in fact, her own long-lost daughter! And great rejoicing, exultation, merriment and wonder filled the house of Joseph, and the entire land of Egypt, on that most auspicious day.

And all who heard of these strange and miraculous things came devoutly to praise the omnipotent and all-wise God of Heaven—God, the merciful and compassionate—to whom alone be highest glory and endless praise forever and ever! Amen.